HOME DRYING
Vegetables
Fruits &
Herbs

by PHYLLIS HOBSON

A Garden Way Guide
of HOMESTEAD RECIPES

GARDEN WAY PUBLISHING
CHARLOTTE, VERMONT, 05445

All rights reserved—no part of this book may be reproduced in any form without permission in writing from the publisher, except by reviewer who wishes to quote brief passages in connection with a review written for inclusion in magazine or newspaper.

Library of Congress Catalog Card Number: 7-12661

ISBN 0-88266-048-9

COPYRIGHT 1975 BY GARDEN WAY PUBLISHING CO.

Third Printing, September 1975

Designed by Frank Lieberman
PRINTED IN THE UNITED STATES

DRYING FOODS

Of all the methods of preserving food, drying is the simplest and most natural. It is also the least expensive, in energy expended, equipment and in storage space.

Compared to canning, which requires special lids and processing equipment and a great deal of shelf space, or freezing, which requires special containers and a constant source of electricity, drying foods is the least complicated method of storing food for the winter months. You simply cut the food into small pieces and spread it out in the sun. When the drying is completed, you put it into a small container — almost any container — and store it in a cool, dark place.

Let's say you have a bushel of green peppers. If you freeze them, that bushel will require at least three cubic feet of freezer space, six to 12 plastic containers (depending on how you cut them) and electricity to keep the peppers frozen until used. The top quality life of frozen peppers is three to six months.

You decide this is too expensive. But if you can them you will need 15 to 20 quart canning jars, 15 to 20 new lids, a pressure canner and more than two hours' processing time, figuring on three loads. From there on, until you use them, you'll need up to two square feet of shelf space for storage of up to one year.

And the quality and convenience of canned peppers is not very high. They lose much of their Vitamin C and often develop a slightly bitter taste. As for convenience, it is seldom that a family can use up a quart of green peppers, yet to can them in pints or half pints would require more jars, more lids, more processing time and more shelf space.

But if you dry this same bushel of peppers, you need very little preparation time. Peppers need not be blanched. You just remove the seeds and stems as you would for freezing or canning, then cut them into small pieces. Now spread the pieces out on cheesecloth-lined trays and place them in the sun.

After two to three days of soaking up the sunshine (which also enriches them nutritionally), the chopped peppers have shriveled to less than one-tenth of their original size and are almost weightless. The entire bushel of peppers will now fit into one quart jar which weighs one-fourth as much as a jar of canned peppers and will take up one-fourth of a square foot of shelf space.

As for convenience, there is no thawing, no unsealing of jars, no leftovers. Simply take out what you need and reclose the jar. Then you re-constitute the food in the simple ways described in the cooking section starting on page 36, and use them for tasty and nutritious dishes.

In all methods of food preservation, the spoilage microorganisms must be arrested in their growth or killed to prevent their multiplying. In canning, the food is heated to kill bacteria, then sealed to prevent recontamination. In drying, the water is removed so that bacteria, mold and yeast have nothing on which to survive.

For home use there are two main methods of dehydrating food: in the sun or with artificial heat. In hot, dry weather sun drying is the simplest, most natural method of food preservation. Many believe it is the most healthful.

Because of the cost of artificial heat, sun drying is recommended except in cases of emergency. It is usually possible to arrange the drying schedule for the normally dry months of July and August.

The equipment needn't be elaborate. For sun drying almost any flat surface will do. You can make a screen-shelved rack for use in the oven with a little hardware cloth (a type of metal screening) and a few pieces of wood. We also have included instructions for making a top-of-the-stove drier that will last for years.

It is possible to dry foods successfully on a wire rack or strung on cord over such sources of artificial heat as a hot water heater, a furnace (in fall or winter) or under five or six 100-watt light bulbs. At average electric rates this might cost 60 cents or so to dry a batch of peppers.

One of Grandmother's favorite spots — just above and behind the wood burning kitchen range — is almost perfect if you are lucky enough to have such luxury equipment. Foods such as beans and corn will dry on a tray set on a register or radiator. You can dry in your oven, too — at about 150 degrees.

But by far the easiest, least complicated place to dry most foods is by the sun on a cloth-covered tray set on the roof of a low building, far enough up to be out of the reach of predators but close enough to the kitchen to check it.

In order to avoid the formation of mold or spoilage over long storage periods, foods must be thoroughly dried, with no hint of moisture in the centers. The length of time required to accomplish this varies with the type of food, the humidity of the air and the amount of heat available, whether natural or artificial. As a general guide, under low humidity and ideal conditions small pieces of fruits and vegetables usually will dry in two to three days in the hot summer sun.

That's days, not nights. Food not only will not dry out on that roof at night, it will re-absorb the moisture it lost during the day, from the condensation and dew. When sun-drying, be prepared to take the trays in at night.

However you dry food, it is best, whenever practical, to cut it into small, thin pieces for faster drying.

A HOMEMADE TOP-OF-THE-STOVE DRIER

Every farm had one of these handy little utensils, which usually were called corn dryers.

If you have access to welding equipment you can make a sturdy, efficient top-of-the-stove food drier in an afternoon. It could be soldered together, but then don't inadvertantly let it get too hot. You can have it made at the nearest sheet metal shop. The drier in effect is a large, shallow double boiler in which heat from hot water held in the bottom pan dries food in the top pan.

You'll need two rectangular pieces of 22-gauge galvanized sheet metal. One piece should be about 26 by 32 inches, the other 30 by 36 inches. A drier this size will fit four burners on the average gas or electric kitchen range or about two-thirds of the top of a wood-burning range, where it can be best used.

Cut a 3-inch square from each corner of the 30 by 36-inch piece like this:

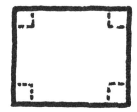

Now cut a 1-inch square from each corner of the 26 by 32-inch piece like this:

Using a length of solid wood to keep the edges straight and a wooden mallet, bend all four edges of each piece like this:

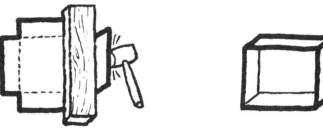

Bend to 45 degrees the small 3 x 3 pieces of metal you cut off in Step 1, and weld them over the four corners of the larger pan to reinforce and strengthen the corners. Using another strip of metal 2 inches wide by 24 inches long, bend it at a 45-degree angle and weld it on the inside of the larger, bottom pan to form a platform for the smaller tray to rest on.

In one corner of the smaller sheet, cut a one-inch hole like this:

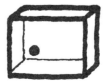

Weld the four corners to form a shallow pan. Using a small strip of folded metal, weld a small fence across the corner to keep the food from falling in the hole. Like this:

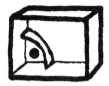

Now set the smaller pan inside the larger pan and weld a folded strip of metal over the top edges of the two pans, making one large pan.

You now have a food drier that will last for years. It is designed mainly for use on a wood-burning kitchen range or laundry stove, in which case a very low fire is kept burning, so that it does not steam. It may be used as a sun drying tray and will speed up the process considerably. To use it, pour hot water into it through the small hole in the bottom pan and spread the food to be dried on the cheesecloth-covered top pan. If the tray is kept in the sun on a summer day, the water will stay warm enough to help dry the food. At the end of the day, lift off the cheesecloth and empty the water from the bottom pan. The next day, refill the pan with hot water.

GENERAL DIRECTIONS

FOR SUN AND ARTIFICIAL DRYING

After being washed, trimmed and cut, the foods to be dried are spread one layer deep on racks or trays. As the foods dry, stir the pieces from time to time to keep them from forming clumps, and to allow the pieces to dry evenly.

Once or twice a day is enough. Larger pieces must be turned separately, but small pieces and such vegetables as peas and beans may be stirred with a spoon or the hands.

And don't forget, each afternoon just before sundown, take the trays inside.

When foods look thoroughly dry, test by cutting a few samples through the center. Look for a darker, wet color and taste for a moist interior which will indicate the food needs a longer drying period.

There are color and texture characteristics to look for: apples, peaches and apricots should be pliable and leathery; peas should be shriveled and wrinkled; corn should be dimpled and semi-transparent; green beans should have a greenish-black color with a limp, leathery texture. Dried foods, in the dried state, do not have a very appetizing appearance.

Before being put into long-term storage, dried foods should be tested for moisture. To do so, pack loosely in glass jars and close the lids tightly. Place in a cool, dark place for two to three days. Then check. If there are small beads of moisture or a definite fogging up inside the jar, the food is not thoroughly dry and should go back on the drying trays. If there are no problem signs the jars may be labeled with the name of the food and the date, and placed in permanent storage. Properly dried foods will keep for several years.

BLANCHING

To blanch or not to blanch is as much discussed in drying as it is in freezing. Proponents say blanching — plunging the food into boiling water for 3 to 5 minutes to stop enzyme action, then into cold water to stop the cooking — is important to long storage life of dried foods. Opponents say it is a waste of time and vitamins.

We've tried it both ways and for us it's a matter of judgement. Some foods you do blanch; some foods you don't. We never blanch fruits (including peppers and tomatoes), but we always blanch peas and greens (spinach, chard, etc.). Sometimes we blanch corn (when it's cut from the cob while fresh and juicy), and beans (immature ones, such as baby limas). Directions are given here for the ways we have found best.

Steam blanching saves more of the nutritive values and gives a better-tasting product, but is less reliable than water blanching. Water blanching can be done in approximately two thirds the time required for steam blanching.

To steam blanch the vegetable is arranged loosely in cheesecloth or in a wire basket on a rack above one or two inches of rapidly boiling water. The lid is put on the vessel and a constant active head of steam is maintained during the entire blanching process. Be sure to allow space for the steam to circulate around and through the pieces of vegetables.

To water blanch allow one gallon of boiling water for each pound of vegetable. (Two gallons for each pound of leafy vegetable.) The vegetable is put into a cheesecloth bag or wire basket and immersed in the boiling water for the length of time required for that vegetable. Water blanching requires only two-thirds the time needed for steam blanching. If a recipe calls for six minutes of steam blanching, for instance, four minutes of water blanching will do.

Either water or steam blanching may be used for any of the recipies following. For variety, and because many people who prefer to sun dry believe it is more natural to sun dry without blanching, we have omitted the blanching process from the sun drying recipes (with a few exceptions), and included it in the recipes using artificial heat. Because we prefer it, we have specified steam blanching, but water blanching may be used if you wish to.

STORING   Almost any container which excludes the air, moisture and insects and protects the food from predators is a good container for dried foods. Use whatever you have on hand in the way of glass jars or metal cans. Just be sure the lids fit tightly if you live in a humid climate. We have successfully used peanut butter and pickle jars that cannot be used for canning, coffee cans fitted with plastic lids, peanut and shortening cans and lard and honey tins with metal lids — almost any kind of container with a tight lid. Don't use paper or plastic bags. Insects soon find their way inside them.

One old-time method of storing dried foods was to pack the food loosely in ordinary brown paper bags, tie the opening with string and hang the bags from a rope strung across the attic. We haven't tried this method but don't recommend it. It sounds like a method almost guaranteed to expose the dried food to the moisture in the air, flying and crawling insects and even rope-walking mice. Once you have packed the dried foods in closed containers, store them on a shelf in a dark, cool closet or cabinet.

SUN DRYING   Centuries ago, before canning jars or freezers were invented, the American Indians preserved their fruits, vegetables and meats for winter by drying them in the sun. Many people believe that drying foods this way saves more of the natural nutrients.

Because most of the water content is removed, dried fruits and vegetables have a substantially increased concentration of vitamins and minerals. The only vitamins lost in sun drying are some of the A and C.

Almost any food can be dried in the sun under the proper conditions of sun and humidity. Some of the easiest are apples, peaches, apricots, plums, cherries, peas, rhubarb, beans and corn.

YOU'll NEED: DRYING TRAYS OR RACKS — Shallow cake trays, cookie sheets, discarded cafeteria dish trays, even boards, make satisfactory drying trays. Or you can make wire racks of screening or hardware cloth, of sheet metal or metal roofing. If it's clean or can be cleaned, almost anything flat will do.

A ROOF — Or at least a place to set the trays while drying. A table top will do but a low roof is best, preferably near the kitchen door for frequent checking. The ground is too vulnerable to people, pets and shade.

OR: — A hotbed or coldframe sash. Not only does the glass cut down on the drying time by concentrating the heat of the sun, but the food is protected from animals and insects without the bother of climbing up to a roof. No need to carry trays inside at night, either. Just close the sash at sundown.

THIN MATERIAL — A cheap grade of cheesecloth or netting is good, but old, freshly-laundered curtains will do. The idea is to line the trays and cover the food to protect it from flies, yet let the rays and heat of the sun come through, and the moisture escape.

LOTS OF SUNSHINE — Fortunately, long, sunny days and the harvest season come at the same time of year.

Apples:

Select firm, mature fruit. Winesap, Jonathan, Russet, Newton, Rome Beauty and Golden Delicious are good varieties. Peel, trim, core and remove bruises. Cut into slices ¼-inch thick and drop into cold salted water (4 tablespoons salt to 1 gallon of water) to keep from browning. Prepare only enough for one tray at a time and spread slices one slice deep, on cheesecloth-lined trays or hardware cloth racks. Place in the hot sun before preparing the next tray.

Examine and stir slices from time to time. Fruit is ready to store when a handful separates at once when squeezed, then released. Slices should have an elastic feel and leave no moisture in the hand. Dried apples should be rubbery and chewy, not hard or crisp.

OR:

Wash, peel and core apples. Dip in ascorbic acid solution to keep from darkening. Lay the slices on a large piece of cheesecloth (or an old, clean curtain) and baste each slice to the cloth with cotton thread, taking a stitch through each slice. Suspend the cloth on the clothesline or tack another piece over the slices and tie to stakes in the sun.

Apricots:

Pick fruit when ripe enough to drop. Wash whole and split in halves, removing the seed. Do not peel. Spread, cut side up, on trays in the sun. Take inside each night until they have a leathery look and feel, with no soft interior.

OR:

Wash, halve and slice ripe apricots. Spread, one layer deep, on cheesecloth-lined trays. Will dry in two to three days, depending on the humidity.

Bananas:

When bananas are brown-flecked ripe, remove skins and slice very thinly. Spread slices on wire racks or cheesecloth-covered trays and dry in the sun. Store slices in tightly-covered jars.

Beans:

If the weather is dry, it is simple to dry beans (navy, kidney, butter, great northern, etc.) right in the garden. Just let them ripen, then dry, right in the pod, on the vine. When the plant and the pod are dry and shriveled, pull the vines, pluck off the pods and find a cool spot under a shade tree. There, at your leisure, thresh or open the pods and shell the dry beans. If the weather has been good and they have dried thoroughly in the garden, the beans can be put in jars to store immediately. If there are some not thoroughly dry, spread them out on trays to finish drying in the sun.

If the weather is wet and you see signs of mold on some bean pods before the beans inside are dry, pull the plants and hang them, upside down, in a shed or dry place until the pods are dry and shriveled. The dry beans then may be shelled.

OR:

Let beans reach full maturity on the vine. When the pods turn yellow, pick them and spread the pods on drying racks and let dry in the sun. When perfectly dry and shriveled, shell the beans and store in jars.

OR:

Pick and shell the ripe beans when they have reached

maturity, but before they have started to dry. Spread on drying trays and place in the sun each day until thoroughly dry. Store in closed containers.

Beets:
Cook whole young beets in water to cover just until skins will slip off — about 20 minutes. Slip off skins, cut off tops and root ends and chop into small (¼-inch) cubes. Chill, then spread thinly on drying trays or cloth-covered wire racks. Sun dry.

Blueberries:
Spread thinly on drying trays and dry in the sun.

Candied Dried Fruits:
Prepare cherries, pineapple, citron or orange or grapefruit rind. Wash, pit and remove any white membrane. Cook in medium syrup (2 cups sugar to 2 cups water) for two hours, or until fruit is clear. Drain and place on platters or drying racks. Dry in the sun. When thoroughly dry, sprinkle with sugar and pack in layers in tins lined with waxed paper. Keep tins tightly closed. May be used for cookies, fruit cakes and candy.

Carrots:
Scrub carrots and slice off ends. Scrape or peel only if necessary. Slice into thin slices and cook in small amount of water only until slices begin to get tender. Drain. Spread out on chilled drying sheets to cool. Dry in the sun.

OR:
Proceed as above, but dry without cooking. The result is a chewier textured product. Good for vegetable soups.

Cherries:

For sweetest flavor, wait to pick when cherries reach dark red, fully-ripe stage. But watch them carefully or the birds will pick them first. Wash and pit, then spread on cheesecloth-lined trays. Cover with a layer of cheesecloth or netting to protect them from the birds. In hot sun, cherries will dry in a day or two.

Corn:

There are almost as many ways to dry corn as there are uses for this versatile vegetable-grain. Here are a few:

Dried sweet corn is delicious cooked as a vegetable. The ears must be gathered in the milk stage and processed immediately, as it deteriorates rapidly. Husk, trim and remove any bad spots. Cut from the cob, being careful not to cut into the cob. Spread on trays ¼-inch deep and stir several times during drying.

OR:

Cut four quarts of corn from the cob. Combine with 3 tablespoons sugar, 4 teaspoons salt and cup cream. Cook over medium heat for 15 minutes, stirring constantly. Spread on cookie sheets or drying trays and dry 1 to 2 days in the sun. Store in air-tight containers.

OR:

Plunge immature corn on the cob in boiling water for three minutes. Remove, chill in cold water and hang up the ears in a dry room where there is free circulation of air. When perfectly dry, shell the corn from the cob and store in glass jars.

OR:

For use as a grain (See cornbread recipe on Page 40), corn may be dried right on the cob. Simply leave a few of the ears in the garden until garden-plowing time in the fall. Then pluck the partially-dried ears, pull back the husks and hang them, upside down, in a dry shed. Be sure to hang them beyond the reach of mice. When the kernels are hard and semi-transparent, twist the cobs in your hands to loosen the kernels, and shell. Store kernels in air-tight containers.

Currants:
Add one pint of sugar to each pint of currants. Combine in a kettle and bring to a boil over low heat. Sugar will dissolve and turn to syrup. Skim off currants and spread on sheets to dry in the sun. Syrup may be used for jelly. Currants may be used as a substitute for raisins.

Figs:
Select perfect, ripe figs. Wash thoroughly. Make a syrup of equal parts sugar and water. Boil 10 minutes, then drop in figs and cook over low heat, stirring to keep from burning, for 40 to 50 minutes, or until fruit is clear. Drain, place on trays in the sun for several days, turning every day. Spread in single layers and bring indoors at night.

Mock Figs (tomatoes):
Scald and skin small, pear-shaped or cherry tomatoes. To 8 pounds tomatoes, add 3 pounds brown sugar. Cook without water over low heat until sugar dissolves and penetrates the tomatoes, giving them a clear appearance. Remove tomatoes, spread on trays in the sun and sprinkle on a little syrup as they dry. When dry, pack in jars or tins, layering with a sprinkling of powdered sugar. Use as for figs.

Garlic:
Wait to pull garlic until the tops fall over. Then pull and lay beside the rows to dry a few hours in the sun. Spread on

racks in the shade of a shed or any open building where there is good circulation of air but no sun. When tops are dry and brittle, braid tops to form a chain. Hang in attic or storage room. (See also section on Herbs.)

Green Beans:

Wash, trim and cut French-style or in one-inch pieces. Dry on trays in the sun until greenish-black and leathery. Turn with a spatula each day.

OR:

Leave green beans whole. Using a large needle and thin cord or string, string tips of beans as you would beads, leaving ½-inch air space between beans. Hang to dry from the clothesline posts.

Lemon Peel:

For wintertime lemon flavoring for apple pies, fish and cakes: each time you use a lemon in the summer, finely grate the yellow of the skin and dry it in the sun a few hours. Collect in a glass jar for winter use.

Lima Beans:

Gather lima beans before they ripen, while the beans are still green and immature in the pods. Shell the beans and spread on cloth-covered trays to dry in the sun.

Mushrooms:

Remove stems but do not wash. String on a long cord, using a darning needle or trussing needle and being careful not to split the mushrooms. Hang in the sun in a good breeze. Store in a wooden box lined with tissue paper. Keep in a dry place and check occasionally for insects.

OR:

Chop mushrooms, stems and all, into fine pieces. Spread on

cheesecloth-covered trays and dry in the sun. Store in covered glass jars.

Onions:
Onions will keep for several months when cured according to the recipe for garlic. However, if you would like the convenience of dried onion flakes on your pantry shelf, peel onions and shred or grate, then spread on cheesecloth-lined racks or trays. Onion flakes will dry thoroughly in one day in the sun, but should be covered with fastened-down cheesecloth or netting to keep the drying flakes from blowing away.

Parsley:
Select large curly parsley and plunge each piece in boiling water, one at a time. Shake thoroughly and hang in an airy place in the sun. When perfectly dry, put in tin boxes between pieces of waxed paper and keep in a dry place.

OR:
Wash and shake the water from each piece of fresh parsley. Place on cheesecloth-covered drying racks and cover with another piece of cheesecloth. Dry in the sun. When perfectly dry, crumble the leaves and discard the stems. Store crumbled leaves in jars.

Parsnips:
Peel by scraping and cut off ends. Slice and cook until tender in small amount of water. Drain. Spread on drying trays and dry in the sun until pliable and wrinkled. Store in jars.

Peaches:
Peaches are best for drying when juicy ripe. Select only the

best, using any with brown spots immediately and drying those that are perfect and golden ripe. Wash the skins and cut in halves or slices, removing the pit. Do not peel. Spread thinly on cheesecloth-lined trays and place in the hot sun. Halves will dry in four to five days; slices in three to four days, depending on the humidity.

Pears:

Pears must be ripe but also firm. Bartlett pears are recommended for drying. Wash and peel, cut in halves and cut out cores. Place on trays, core side up, and dry in the hot sun in a well-ventilated place. Will take four to five days.

Peas:

Pick when peas are at their green best. Carefully pick over and remove any pods that are mildewed or spotted. Do not wash. Spread pods on trays or racks in the sun. After several days, the peas inside the pods will be so dry you can hear them rattle when you shake them. Shell and store peas in clean, dry jars.

OR:

Gather garden peas when in perfect condition for table use, not yellowed or dried. Immerse pods in boiling water for 3 minutes. Shell the peas and dip for 1 or 2 minutes in boiling water containing two tablespoons salt to the gallon. Drain and spread thinly on trays. Stir occasionally as they dry. When ready for storage, the peas should be uniformly dry throughout and show no moisture in the center when split.

Peppers:

Small, hot peppers may be strung whole on twine by threading with a large-eyed needle. Large, sweet peppers may be washed, cut in half and seeded, then strung in the same way. Both may be hung on a clothesline or in any sunny, airy spot.

OR:

To peel, plunge whole sweet peppers — either green or red — in boiling water for one minute. Then cool in ice water and slip off skins. Cut out core and remove seeds. Chop into ¼-inch pieces and spread on drying trays and place in the sun. Will dry in less than a day. Convenient for adding to casseroles and meat dishes.

Plums:

Plums are dried whole, without pitting or blanching. Wash, then spread on trays. Drying will take a few days.

Prunes:

Prune plums should be allowed to ripen until they fall from the tree. Do not remove stones. Dip in boiling water, submerging the fruit one to two minutes to kill any insects or eggs. Spread in a single layer on the trays. Prunes are dry when the flesh shows no moisture and has attained the typical chewy texture of prunes.

Pumpkin:

The firm, deep-colored pie pumpkin varieties are best for drying. Peel and cut into strips two inches wide. Remove strings and seeds and cut into pieces about ½-inch thick. Steam five minutes. Cool and spread on trays in the sun. Pumpkin is dry when pieces are leathery, but show no moisture when cut and crushed. Store in air-tight containers.

OR:

Slice into three-to-four inch pieces, discarding the stringy pulp and seeds. Bake or steam until soft, then squeeze through a colander or run through blender. Dry in the sun on an earthenware plate covered to a depth of one inch. Break into pieces and store in tins or jars.

Raspberries:
Pick over berries, removing stems. Spread on trays one layer deep and place in the sun to dry. When thoroughly dry (cut a few samples to check), may be stored in air-tight jars or cans.

Rhubarb:
Wash rhubarb stalks. With a sharp knife, strip off outer skin to aid drying. Cut into two-inch pieces and dry on trays.

OR:
Wash and cut stalks into one-inch pieces, then string, bead fashion, on a thin cord. Hang to dry in a breezy spot in full sun. Check for moisture around the cord before storing.

Rutabaga:
Peel and cut off ends. Cut into chunks and bake, covered, until tender. Mash with a fork or potato masher or run through a blender until puréed. Spread out on drying tray lined with butcher paper or on an earthenware plate. Dry two days, until it has a pliable, leathery texture, then break into pieces and dry one more day.

Soybeans:
Soybeans are best dried in the garden as navy or great northern beans. Leave them on the vines until the stalks and leaves are completely dried and brown, then thresh by hand or shell them as you would peas. Do not pick soybeans green for drying.

Squash:

Summer squash, such as yellow squash and zucchini, may be washed and sliced thinly without peeling, and the slices spread on cheesecloth-lined trays for drying.

OR:

Summer squash may be steamed and forced through a colander or blender, then spread on trays to dry. When thoroughly dry, break into pieces or pound into a powder before storing.

OR:

Winter squash may be steamed or baked and dried as above or it may be cut into chunks or strips and dried as for pumpkin.

Strawberries:

Wash, stem and discard any over-ripe berries. For best flavor, strawberries should be mixed with an equal amount of dry sugar to bring out juice, then spread on trays to dry in the sun. Stir occasionally to keep separated. Store in glass jars.

OR:

Wash, stem and sort berries and spread on trays, then dribble with a mild-flavored honey. Stir frequently with a spoon or knife until thoroughly dry.

Tomatoes:

Peel fully-ripened tomatoes by plunging them for two minutes in boiling water, then for two minutes in cold water. Slip off skins, cut out cores and squeeze slightly to remove part of the juice. (Save it for drinking or soup.) Cut in halves and lay on trays, cut side up, in the sun. Turn frequently and put on fresh trays occasionally, if necessary, to avoid the accumulation of excess juice. Store in jars or cans.

OR:

Remove skins and cores from ripe tomatoes and chop into ½-inch pieces. Drain off juice into dish and save for other uses. Drain two hours, then spread chopped tomatoes on trays to dry.

Turnips:

Wash, cut off ends and drain or wipe dry. Cut into thin slices and spread on drying trays. Store in glass jars.

DRYING WITH ARTIFICIAL HEAT

On Page 6 we give instructions for making a top-of-the-stove drier of the type midwestern farmers have used for generations. If you have soldering or welding equipment, you can make it yourself. If not, you can have it made reasonably.

Or, if you have an oven with a dependable thermostat and a low temperature range, you may dry foods in the oven. Just turn the heat as low as possible and open the door somewhat for air circulation. To cut costs, take advantage of a warm oven, after baking foods, or the heat left in electric burners after food has been cooked. Just be sure the temperature is not above 150 degrees, which tends to cook the food and destroy vitamins.

There are other possibilities — over a furnace register, behind the refrigerator, almost any place where the temperature is between 100 and 150 degrees and there is circulation of air.

While drying with artificial heat is not as natural or healthful as sun drying, it is sometimes necessary in an emergency, such as when the rains come at harvest time.

But ovens and top-of-the-stove driers are limited in size, unlike shed roofs, which will hold many drying trays. While a top-of-the-stove drier or an oven will dry a trayful of vegetables in a few hours, they will not accommodate the volume of food that may be dried by the sun in a day or two.

General Directions:
Wash, trim and slice or cube vegetables and fruit. Some fruits, such as apricots and plums, are left whole or cut in half, but in general, thin strips or diced pieces dry faster and keep better than thick chunks.

SOME RECIPES FOR DRYING WITH ARTIFICIAL HEAT

Apples:
Peel, trim and core crisp, tart apples. Cut into thin slices and dip in cold salt water (4 tablespoons salt to a gallon of water). Drain and spread thinly on top-of-the-stove drier or on a wire rack in a 110 to 150-degree oven. Dry until apples are elastic and chewy, but with no moisture.

OR:

Peel, trim, core and slice apples. Cook in a small amount of water until slices break up and become a thick sauce. Pour in a thin layer on top-of-the-stove drier or on a drying tray and place in 150-degree oven. Dry, stirring every few hours until firm and chewy. The drier you get it, the longer it will keep. Cut in strips, hang strips in a well-ventilated spot 24 hours, then roll up and store in jars.

Apricots:

Wash and split ripe apricots, removing pits. Spread on top-of-the-stove drier or on cookie sheets or wire racks, cut side down in a 120 to 150-degree oven. If weather is dry, remove from heat and hang in cheesecloth sling or strung on cord like beads for 24 hours. Apricots are dry when the pieces are leathery feeling and chewy when eaten.

Beans:

Pull pods of navy, kidney, pinto, or great northern beans when pods begin to yellow. Shell beans immediately to avoid mildew. Spread shelled beans thinly on top-of-the-stove drier or on drying trays in a warm (150-degree) oven. Leave oven door slightly ajar.

Beets:

Pull beets when about two inches in diameter. Wash and cook until done in boiling water to cover. Slip off skins and cut into thin slices or small cubes. Spread on trays at 1½ pounds to the square foot. Dry on top-of-the-stove drier or in an oven on low heat until brittle.

Blueberries:

Spread washed blueberries in single layer on top-of-the-stove drier.

Carrots:

Pull when the visible top portion is about ½-inch in diameter. Wash and peel or scrape. Cut in thin lengthwise or crosswise slices. Steam 5 to 7 minutes. Spread on top-of-the-stove drier at 1½ pounds to the square foot. Dry over low heat.

Cherries:

Spread washed, pitted cherries on top-of-the-stove drier. Dry over low heat.

Corn:

Blanch whole ears by plunging in boiling water 3 minutes, then quickly chill in cold water. Cut kernels from cob and spread on top-of-the-stove drier. Dry over low heat and store in glass jars.

Currants:

Currants may be sweetened as with sun drying or may be dried whole and unsweetened, like blueberries. Dry on top-of-the-stove drier.

Figs:

Cook figs over low heat for about one hour, adding sugar or honey to taste. Stir occasionally and cook to a thick paste then spread in a very thin layer on a greased cookie sheet. Dry in a low oven until chewy. Cut in strips and hang in the kitchen 24 hours, then sprinkle with sugar and roll up. Store in glass jars.

Green Beans:

Pick pods while immature, before the beans inside have developed. Wash and cut in one-inch lengths or French style (cut diagonally or lengthwise). Steam one-inch lengths 8 to 10 minutes; French style 3 to 5 minutes. Spread at rate of 1 pound per square foot on top-of-the-stove drier. Dry until limp and leathery.

Lima Beans:

Pick while still green and immature. Shell without washing. Steam 8 to 10 minutes and place on top-of-the-stove drier, spread at the ratio of one pound per square foot. Dry until hard and wrinkled.

Parsley:
Spread chopped parsley on top-of-the-stove drier or in 120 to 150-degree oven. Store in glass jars.

Peaches:
Cut fresh, ripe peaches in half. Remove pits. Place cut side down on top-of-the-stove drier or cut side up on drying racks in oven. Dry until peach halves are chewy and leathery, with no moisture in the centers when cut. In dry weather, hang in cheesecloth slings 24 hours before storing.

Pears:
Peel and halve very ripe pears. Cut out cores with measuring spoon and sharp knife. Leave in halves or cut into ½-inch pieces. Spread on wire racks and place in warm oven or top-of-the-stove drier. Turn occasionally and dry until leathery feeling and chewy.

Peas:
Pick before peas are quite ripe, when they just begin to fill the pods. Shell, discarding any yellowed peas. Blanch 6 to 10 minutes and spread, 1 pound to the square foot, on top-of-the-stove drier or oven drying racks. Dry until hard and wrinkled.

Peppers:
Wash sweet green or red peppers and cut in half. Remove stem and seeds and white center membrane. Chop into small, cooking-size pieces and spread on top-of-the-stove drier or oven drying trays. When perfectly dry, store in glass jars.

Pumpkin:
Cut firm, ripe pumpkin into 1-inch strips. Peel and remove

strings and seeds from each strip. Cut into small pieces and steam 5 minutes. Spread on wire racks and dry in oven or on top-of-the-stove drier. Store in jars.

OR:

Cut large pumpkin in half and remove strings and seeds from each half. Bake in 300-degree oven until meat is soft. Scrape meat from shell and force through colander or blender. Add 1½ cups honey or raw sugar and 2 teaspoons cinnamon for each quart of pumpkin pulp. Stir well. Pour out on drying trays and dry in oven or on top-of-the-stove drier until pumpkin is chewy. Cut in strips, hang 24 hours, then roll each strip in waxed paper and store in a glass jar.

Raspberries:
Pick over berries, remove stems. Spread on trays one layer deep and place in top-of-the-stove drier or in warm oven. Store in glass jars or cans.

Rhubarb:
Wash stalks and strip off outer skin. Cut into small pieces and spread on trays to dry in top-of-the-stove drier or in oven.

Soybeans:
Pick when ripe. Blanch the pods in steam 5 to 7 minutes, then shell. Spread at 1 pound to the square foot on drying trays or in top-of-the-stove drier. Dry until hard and wrinkled.

OR:

Soybeans may be spread on drying trays and toasted in 200-degree oven like peanuts, then sealed in glass jars to eat as snacks.

Squash:

Summer squash may be washed and sliced thinly without peeling and dried in a top-of-the-stove drier or in a low heat oven.

Strawberries:

Wash, stem and slice ripe berries. Spread thinly on top-of-the-stove drier or in oven drying trays. Dry until all hint of moisture is gone. Store in glass jars.

Tomatoes:

Slice ripe tomatoes in very thin slices. Place on a cloth-covered cookie sheet and dry in a low (150-degree) oven. Turn frequently to prevent sticking.

OR:

Peel ripe tomatoes by blanching 2 minutes. Slip off skins, cut out core and squeeze out excess juice. Cut meat into thin slices or small pieces and dry in top-of-the-stove drier or on trays in oven.

OR:

Proceed as above, but instead of cutting tomatoes, force through colander or blender. Pour onto drying trays and dry. Break into pieces and chop or grind into powder. Store in jars.

Turnips and Rutabagas:

Wash and drain. Slice very thin. Steam slices 6 to 10 minutes, then chill. Spread on top-of-the-stove drier or on drying trays 1 pound to the square foot. Dry until brittle.

Almost any meat may be dried provided it is lean (trim off any trace of fat to avoid rancidity) and fresh. Slice meat into very thin slices to allow it to dry quickly, and store it in a tightly-covered container in a dark place.

Dried Beef or Ham:

Roast slowly in a 300-degree oven to the just-done stage. Cover to keep from forming a crust. When done, chill overnight in the coldest part of the refrigerator.

When chilled to the almost-frozen stage, slice as thin as possible on the thinnest setting of a meat slicer or with a very sharp knife. Keep meat chilled as you work.

Spread slices on drying racks which have been covered with parchment paper (not plastic coated) and dry in the oven (sun drying or top-of-the-stove drying are not recommended). Be certain meat is dry before storing.

Brined Dried Beef:

For longer keeping qualities, make a brine of 2 gallons boiling water, 6 cups pickling salt and 2 cups sugar. Dissolve and cool. Pour over 10 pounds of raw beef placed in a heavy crock. Place a weight on the meat to keep it covered by the brine and keep in a cool place 48 hours. Remove from liquid, slice very thin and dry in the sun or a 150-degree oven.

Dried Cured Beef:

Mix 1 cup pickling salt and ½ cup sugar. Use 1/3 of this mixture to rub over 10 pounds of beef cut into 6-inch pieces, 2 inches thick. Use about ½ cup and rub in well, being sure not to miss any of the surface. Pack meat closely in a crock and cover with a towel, tied on. Refrigerate or keep in a very cool place for 3 days.

Then rub with another 1/3 of the mixture and repack in the crock, this time putting at the bottom the pieces which were on top. Leave the liquid which has accumulated in the crock. Three days later, repeat, using the last 1/3 of the mixture. Repack for another 3 days.

At the end of this period, hang the meat to drip for 24 hours, then slice in very thin slices. Spread slices on drying racks and place in the sun or in a low (not more than 150-degrees) oven. Store in airtight jars.

Dried Venison:
Venison may be dried using any of the recipes for beef.

Dried Cured Pork:
Combine 1 cup pickling salt and ½ cup brown (or raw) sugar. Mix thoroughly, then divide into three equal parts. Rub one part over 10 pounds of lean pork cut into 2-pound chunks. Use about ½ cup, rubbing in well. Pack into a crock, cover and keep in a cool place 4 days. Remove meat from container, rub with the second part of the mixture and repack. Let set 4 days in a cool place. At the end of 4 days, repeat, repacking tightly in crock. Let set in a cool place three weeks, then remove and hang to drip 24 hours. Slice very thinly, then spread on trays to dry in sun or in a very low oven. Store in covered containers.

Dried Fish:
Cut the fish down the back. Skin. Take out entrails and rub the outside and inside well with pickling salt. Hang to drain 24 hours. Combine 1 cup pickling salt and 1 cup brown sugar. Rub the fish well with this, then lay on a board in the sun 24 hours, taking in at night. Rub well again with salt mixture and put it back until thoroughly dry. Store in airtight container.

OR:

Clean and scale fish. Smoke or bake in warm oven to flaky stage. When done, flake meat from bones and spread on drying trays. Dry in 150-degree oven and store in glass jars.

OR:

Small fish may be left whole or split in half and dried without baking or smoking. Sprinkle with salt and dry in 150-degree oven.

Poultry:
Bake or stew mature chicken or turkey. When tender, remove from broth or drippings and chill, covered. When thoroughly chilled, remove skin and all traces of fat, then slice as thin as possible. Spread on parchment-covered drying trays and dry in oven.

Rabbit, Squirrel and other small game:
Clean and roast, covered, in 300-degree oven. Chill. Pull meat from skin and bones and slice very thin. Dry on parchment-covered oven trays.

DRYING MILK AND EGGS

Drying milk and eggs isn't as easy as spreading beans on a tray, but it can be done. Here's how:

Drying Milk:
Bring 2 to 3 inches of water to a boil in a large kettle. Over this, double-boiler style, place a smaller kettle about half full of milk. Simmer several hours, or until much of the water has evaporated from the milk, adding water to the bottom kettle as necessary.

When milk is thick as cream, pour onto drying tray with 2-inch sides and dry in 150-degree oven. When milk is dry, tray can be flexed to flip off the dried milk to a clean towel. When cooled, grind dried milk in meat grinder, grain mill or electric blender, using finest blade or grind. Store in glass jars.

Drying Whole Eggs:
Combine several eggs in a bowl and beat with an egg beater until light. Spread in a thin layer on an earthenware platter or flexible cookie sheet with sides. Dry in a warm oven. Break into pieces and grind in a meat grinder or electric grinder, using the finest blade or highest speed.

Dried Egg Yolk:
Beat egg yolks until light and pour onto earthenware plate. Dry in hot sun or a warm oven, then grind or pound to a powder.

Dried Egg Whites:
Stir egg whites with a spoon and spread out on earthenware plate in the sun or in a warm oven. Dry to brittle stage, then pound to a powder and store in glass jars.

FRUIT PAPERS OR LEATHERS

Sugar always was scarce and expensive for the original homesteaders and sweets were a special treat. To use up their surplus fruit crops and to see them through the long winter months when the sugar barrel was empty, they invented a naturally sweet, chewy fruit concoction which was much more healthful than sugar.

Some families called them "papers." Others called them "leathers." Whatever you call them, they're simple, healthful and delicious.

Apple Leather:

Wash, peel, core and slice cooking apples. Cook, without water, over low heat until slices cook up into a thick applesauce. Spread thinly over earthenware plates or cookie sheets and dry in the sun for two to three days, or until the leather is soft, pliable and chewy, with no moisture inside. Cut into strips, then hang to dry 24 hours. The longer leathers are dried, the longer they will keep. Roll up and store in closed jars.

Apricot Paper:

Slip skins from apricots by dipping in boiling water, then cold water. Then cut in half and remove pits, and cook slowly in just enough water to keep from burning. When fruit is soft, mash with a potato masher or force through a colander. Spread very thin on plates or cookie sheets to dry in the sun. When dry cut into strips, hang for 24 hours, sprinkle with sugar and roll up to store in jars.

Peach Paper:

Peel, pit and mash very ripe peaches. Cook, stirring constantly, over low heat. When quite thick, spread very thin on plates or cookie sheets to dry in the sun. Should be dry in two to three days. Cut into strips, hang for 24 hours, then roll up and store in glass jars.

Plum Leather:

Allow plums to hang on the tree until they are sweet-ripe. Remove pits and skins and cook in their own juice over low heat, stirring frequently. Mash or force through colander and spread thinly on plates or cookie sheets to dry in the sun. Cut into jar-lengths, let hang 24 hours, roll into sticks and store in glass jars.

Mixed Fruit Paper:

Peel, core or pit and cut up any combination of fruits. Cook over low heat, stirring frequently, until fruit is soft and thick. Spread out on plates or cookie sheets and dry in the sun. Cut into jar-length pieces, hang for 24 hours and roll into sticks. Store in jars.

COOKING WITH DRIED FOODS

To dry fruits and vegetables, you removed the water. To restore them you put it back. The method varies with the food, but the purpose is the same for all foods — put back the water you took out.

Usually this is accomplished by soaking. Beans are probably the most familiar dried food. Most people know that dried beans — lima, kidney, navy, great northern, etc. — should be soaked overnight, then cooked for several hours. Many dried foods are prepared the same way.

But many need not be cooked at all. Fruit papers are eaten as is, like candy. Or they may be soaked for a couple of hours, then rolled up and baked in pastry dough for an extra special dessert.

Vegetables such as green beans, peas and corn are soaked three to four hours, then cooked in the same water in which they are soaked to preserve the vitamins. Cook just until done. Green beans cut French style take less soaking and less cooking time than those left whole.

COOKING DRIED FRUITS

Dried Apple Cake:

Soak 3 cups dried apples overnight in warm water. In the morning, drain and chop fine. Simmer two hours in 2 cups thin molasses. Cool and add 2 cups butter, 1 cup sugar, 3 eggs, 1 teaspoon cinnamon, 2 teaspoons ground cloves, ½ teaspoon ground nutmeg, 1 teaspoon allspice and 1 cup sour milk. Combine with 5 cups flour and 4 teaspoons baking soda dissolved in 2 tablespoons hot water. Add 1 cup raisins and 1 cup dried currants. Beat well and bake in a well-greased and floured baking pan in 350-degree oven. If stored in a stone jar will keep for several weeks. (This recipe is more than 100 years old.)

Fried Apples:
Soak ½ pound dried apples overnight in 3 cups boiling water. Drain and sauté with breakfast bacon. Serve hot with bacon and eggs.

Spiced Apples:
Combine 2/3 cup honey, ½ cup vinegar, 1 stick of cinnamon and ¼ teaspoon cloves in a saucepan. Put 1 pound dried apples in a ½-gallon crock or heavy bowl. Bring vinegar-spice mixture to the boiling point and immediately pour over the dried apples. Cover and let set 24 hours. Remove cloves and cinnamon. Eat without cooking for slightly-chewy apple slices or simmer gently one-half hour for applesauce.

Apple-Indian Pudding:
Scald 1 quart milk and pour it over 14 level tablespoons ground dried corn. Cool, then add 1 quart cold milk and 1½ cups chopped dried apples which have been soaked overnight. Add 2/3 cup molasses and 1 teaspoon salt, ½ teaspoon cinnamon and ¼ teaspoon nutmeg. Bake 1 hour in 350-degree oven. Serve with cream.

Dried Apple Pie:
Cover 1½ cups dried apples with 3 cups water and simmer

over low heat until tender. Add ½ cup sugar and 1 teaspoon dried lemon peel. Pour into unbaked pie shell and dot with butter. Sprinkle with ½ teaspoon ground cinnamon. Cover with top crust. Bake in 350-degree oven 30 minutes, or until brown.

Dried Applesauce:

Dried apples may be cooked without soaking if they are simmered over low heat 2 to 3 hours. Add water as needed. Keep covered and stir occasionally. Season with a little lemon juice and add ½ cup currants or raisins to each 2 cups apples.

Dried Berries:

Pour 4 cups cold water over 2 cups dried berries and slowly bring just to the boiling point. Simmer 30 minutes.

Dried Blueberries:

Soak overnight in a small amount of water. Drain and add without cooking to muffin, pancake or cake batter. Also good for pies.

Cherry Batter Pudding:

Combine 2 cups milk, 2 eggs, 1 tablespoon melted butter, ¼ teaspoon salt and 2 teaspoons baking powder. Add enough ground wheat flour to make a thick batter. Add 1 cup dried cherries (without soaking) and stir just to combine. Bake 1 hour in 350-degree oven in which a pan of water provides steam.

Dried Fruit Compote:

Put any combination of dried fruit — dried apples, currants and peaches is good — in a covered dish or crock and just cover fruit with hot water. Put in a 250-degree oven and bake 3 to 4 hours.

Stewed Dried Fruit:

To one pound of dried apples, peaches, pears or plums, add 1½ quarts boiling water and soak overnight. In the morning, simmer until tender, about 30 minutes.

Dried Fruit Mincemeat:

Grind the following with the coarse blade in a food chopper:

2 pounds dried beef or venison, soaked and cooked
1 pound fresh suet
3 pounds dried apples, soaked and chopped
2 pounds dried raisins
1 pound dried currants
1 lemon, pulp and rind, without seeds
1 orange, pulp and rind, without seeds

Add the following and mix well:

4 cups meat stock in which meat was cooked
2 cups vinegar
1 quart apple cider
1½ cups molasses
4 cups brown sugar
2 tablespoons salt
2 teaspoons ground cinnamon

Combine and simmer over low heat for 2 hours, or until thick. Stir often to prevent sticking.

Dried Peach Pie:

Soak 1½ cups dried peaches overnight, then stew until soft, about 1 hour. Chop; add ¼ cup cream and ½ cup sugar. Pour into an unbaked pie crust and top with 1 tablespoon butter. Cover with top crust. Bake 30 to 40 minutes, until a golden brown, in 350-degree oven.

Dried Prunes:

Put 1 pound dried prunes in a ½-gallon crock or heavy mixing bowl. Combine 1 quart boiling water, the juice of one lemon and ½ cup honey. Pour over prunes and cover. Let set 24 hours and they're ready to eat. Store, covered, in the refrigerator.

Dried Rhubarb:

Soak dried rhubarb in water (1 quart water to 1 pound rhubarb) 3 to 4 hours in a covered casserole dish. Pour off any remaining water and add 1 cup sugar for every 2 cups soaked rhubarb. Cover and bake 30 minutes in a 350-degree oven.

COOKING DRIED VEGETABLES

Carrot Pudding:

Soak 1 cup dried carrots overnight. Chop and combine with ¾ pound chopped suet, 1 cup dried raisins and currants, 4 tablespoons sugar, 8 tablespoons flour and 1 teaspoon cinnamon. Steam in a 300-degree oven 4 hours, then brown 20 minutes.

Corn:

To use, soak in a small amount of milk. Then simmer ½ hour over low heat. Add butter and salt to taste.

Cornbread:

1 cup dried corn (freshly ground in food grinder or flour mill or kitchen blender)

1 cup wheat flour	1 cup milk
1/3 cup sugar	1 egg
½ teaspoon salt	¼ cup butter
3 teaspoons baking powder	

Combine dry ingredients. Beat egg and add to milk. Pour into dry mixture, add melted butter and stir just enough to blend. Pour into greased 8-inch square pan and bake in 425-degree oven 25 minutes.

Parsley:
To use, soak in cold water overnight, shake and use the same as fresh parsley.

Pumpkin (pieces):
To use, soak overnight in milk.
(blended strips):
Use like a confection or use for pies by soaking overnight in milk in the refrigerator. Allow ½ cup dried pumpkin in 1½ cups milk for each pie.

Squash, Summer:
To use, soak four hours in water, then dip in egg, then in flour for frying, or slices may be simmered slowly 30 minutes in a small amount of water without soaking.

OR:
Soak slices 3 to 4 hours in water, then dip in batter and fry as fresh squash, or cut into small pieces and force through a colander as pumpkin.

DRIED VEGETABLE SOUPS Because most soups are simmered over low heat for long periods, dried foods need not be soaked before adding. The following recipes are adapted to dried foods:

Bean Soup:
2 cups dried beans (lima, navy, great northern or pinto)
2 tablespoons chopped dried onion

2 tablespoons chopped dried green pepper
6 tablespoons dried tomato
1 small piece dried cured pork or beef

Soak beans and pork in cold water 3 to 4 hours or overnight. Add enough water to cover well and add remaining ingredients. Simmer over low heat about 4 hours, or until beans are tender. Thicken by taking out 1 cup of cooked beans and forcing through a colander, then returning to the soup. Serves 4 to 6.

Dried Pea Soup:
1 cup dried peas
1 tablespoon diced dried onion
¼ cup crushed dried celery leaves
Salt
Pepper
½ cup dried milk
3 tablespoons butter

Put dried vegetables in pan and cover with cold water. Simmer over low heat 3 to 4 hours, until peas are soft. Add dried milk and butter and more water, if needed. Simmer, stirring often, ½ hour longer. Serves 4.

Dried Pea-Tomato Soup:
1 cup dried peas
1 cup dried tomatoes
6 cups water
¼ cup diced dried onion
¼ cup crushed dried celery leaves
Salt
Pepper
1 tablespoon flour
1 tablespoon butter

Cover peas and tomatoes with water. Add onion and celery leaves and simmer over low heat 3 to 4 hours, or until peas are tender. Strain through a sieve or colander, then season with salt and pepper. Add butter and thicken with flour. Serves 4.

Vegetable Soup:
2 cups diced dried beef
6 cups water
½ cup diced dried carrots
½ cup diced dried turnips
¼ cup dried crushed celery leaves
¼ cup diced dried onion
¼ cup dried peas
1 cup dried tomatoes
Salt
12 peppercorns
1 dried bay leaf
3 cloves
2 tablespoons chopped dried parsley
1 sprig dried thyme

Put meat and vegetables in a large cooking pot and cover with cold water. Tie peppercorns, bay leaf and cloves in a small piece of muslin. Add parsley and thyme. Place pot over medium heat and bring almost to a boil. Reduce heat to low and simmer 4 to 6 hours, until vegetables are tender. Season to taste. Remove muslin bag before serving. Serves 6 to 8.

COOKING DRIED MEATS & FISH

Dried Beef and Eggs:
Put ½ pound sliced brined dried beef in a frying pan with just enough water to cover. Bring to a boil and simmer 10 minutes, then drain off water. Cut meat into small bits. Melt two tablespoons butter with the meat, then add four well-beaten eggs. Stir over low heat until eggs are done.

Dried Pork and Eggs:

Soak ½ cup dried pork and ½ cup dried eggs in 2 cups warm water overnight. In the morning, melt 1 tablespoon butter in a small skillet over low heat. Add pork and egg mixture and cook over low heat, stirring occasionally. Serves 4.

Creamed Dried Fish:

Tear ½ cup dried, salted fish into pieces and soak in warm water overnight. Drain and add 1 cup white sauce. Garnish with sliced hard-cooked eggs.

Dried Chicken Soup:

To ½ cup diced dried chicken, add 1 quart water, ¼ cup diced dried carrots, 1 tablespoon diced dried onion, 1 tablespoon crushed dried celery leaves, 2 tablespoons dried peas and 1 teaspoon dried parsley leaves. Simmer over low heat 3 to 4 hours, or until meat and vegetables are tender. Add 1 cup milk, 1 tablespoon butter or chicken fat and salt and pepper to taste. Serves 4.

Dried Fish Bisque:

Soak ½ cup dried salted fish overnight in 2 cups water. Pour off water and cut up fish in small pieces. Cover with 1 quart cold water or chicken broth and add 1 tablespoon butter, 1 teaspoon diced dried onion, 1 teaspoon diced dried green pepper and 1 teaspoon diced dried parsley. Simmer over low heat until fish is tender. Add 1 cup hot milk and thicken with 1 tablespoon flour. Serves 2.

COOKING WITH DRIED EGGS

To use, dissolve 2 tablespoons powdered whole egg in 2½ tablespoons warm water (to equal 1 egg). First add 1 teaspoon warm water to egg powder, stir to smooth paste, add remainder of water, beat smooth.

To use dried egg yolk, add 1 tablespoon warm water to 1½ tablespoons dried yolk to equal one fresh egg yolk.

To use dried whites, sprinkle 1 tablespoon whites into 2 tablespoons warm water. Let stand 15 or 20 minutes, stirring occasionally. Use half and half with fresh egg whites when making meringue or icing where volume is wanted.

COOKING WITH DRIED MILK

To use, add four parts water to one part milk. Let soak one hour, then use for cooking.

BRINING MEATS, VEGETABLES, EGGS & BUTTER

There is yet another method of food preservation — brining — which is simple, convenient and almost foolproof for the homesteader.

Brining is a temporary method of food preservation, to be used only during the cold months when natural temperatures of 30 to 40 degrees can be maintained. Brined foods spoil quickly when temperatures go above 50. Therefore, it's best to brine vegetables in the late fall season.

All that is needed is a supply of salt and a crock or two to preserve meat, vegetables, even eggs and butter in a cold brine solution. Just make the brine and keep the food well under the surface and in a cool, dark place. If a scum forms on the surface, simply skim it off and add some salt to the brine. Keep each food in a separate crock.

Brined Pork:
Cut pork into 1-pound chunks. Rub well with pickling salt

and let stand overnight. Pack tightly in a crock and cover with a brine made of 5 cups pickling salt and 1½ cups brown sugar for each gallon of water. To keep the pork under the brine, place a piece of hardwood over the meat and weigh it down with a clean, heavy rock or a quart jar filled with water. Cover with a cloth and keep the crock in a cool place just above freezing. From time to time check to be sure the meat is always covered by the brine.

Brined Beef or Venison:

Cut meat into convenient-sized pieces, about 5 or 6 inches square. Weigh it. For each 10 pounds of beef or venison, use 2 cups of pickling salt. Sprinkle a thin layer of salt (about ¼ inch) over the bottom of a crock which will hold all the meat. Over the salt pack in closely a layer of beef about six inches thick, then another layer of salt. Repeat until all meat and salt have been used, reserving a layer of salt for the top. Let stand overnight in a cool place, then pour over the salted beef a solution made by dissolving 1 cup sugar and 1 tablespoon baking soda in two quarts of boiling water. Allow to cool, then pour over the meat. To keep the meat covered by the brine place a clean plate over it and weigh it down with a rock or water-filled jar. Cover with a towel and keep in a cold place until ready to use.

Green Beans:

Pick and wash immature green beans. Remove stem end. Pack in stone jars and cover with a brine made by dissolving 3 cups pickling salt in 1 gallon of water. Place a plate and weight on top to keep the beans under the brine. Cover with a clean towel or paper and tie down. Keep in a cold place.

Corn:

Pull ears of corn when slightly overripe but not too hard. Tie the husks tightly with string at the top end. Pack in a clean crock or barrel and cover with a strong brine made by dissolving 3 cups salt in 1 gallon of warm water. Cool before pouring over the corn. Weight down with the ears to keep under the brine and cover with a cloth, tied down. Keep in a cold place. To use, strip husks from the ears and cover with cold water. Bring to a boil over medium heat and pour off water. Repeat until corn loses much of the salt taste as it cooks.

Butter:

Dissolve 3 cups pickling salt in 1 gallon of boiling water. Add ¼ cup sugar and stir until dissolved. Chill until as cold as possible. Pour into earthenware crock. Wrap one-pound pieces of butter in muslin or cheesecloth and tie with a string. Drop into cold brine and weigh down to keep under the liquid. Cover and store in a cold place.

Beets:

Pull small, young beets and cook in hot water just until skins will slip off, about 20 minutes. Cut off tops and roots and slip off skins. Put in earthenware crock to cool. Meanwhile, dissolve 1 cup salt, ½ cup vinegar and ¼ cup sugar in 2 quarts boiling water. Pour over the beets and let cool, then cover and place in a cold room.

Carrots:

Cook very small, young carrots (or larger carrots cut into strips) until almost tender. Drain, cool and place in a crock or jar. Over the carrots pour a solution made by dissolving 1 cup pickling salt, ¼ cup brown sugar and ½ cup vinegar in 2 quarts boiling water. Cool and pour over carrots. Weigh down to keep carrots under the brine, tie paper or cloth over the top and store in a cool place.

Cauliflower:

Cut raw cauliflower into flowerettes. Soak overnight in salt water to remove any insects. Place in a crock and pour over them a brine made by dissolving 1 cup salt in 2 quarts water. If available place a few sprigs of fresh, green dill over the cauliflower. Weigh down and cover with cloth or paper. Store in a cold place.

COOKING BRINED VEGETABLES

Most brined vegetables, such as cauliflower, beets and carrots, are eaten as they come from the crock, like pickles. Green beans and corn, however, must be cooked. To remove the very salty taste, cover them with cold water and bring to a boil, then pour off the water. After 3 to 4 times most of the salt taste is gone. It is also a good idea to cook the vegetable with another food (such as potatoes with green beans) or in a soup, to remove the salt taste.

COOKING BRINED MEAT & FISH

Brined Beef:

Remove a piece or two of beef from the brine crock and wash off salt in running water. Cover with cold water and add 1 teaspoon peppercorns and 4 dried bay leaves. Simmer over very low heat 5 or 6 hours or until meat is very tender. Let set in liquid until cool. Remove any bones and press under a weight to mold into a firm piece for slicing. Discard liquid and serve meat cold.

OR:

Remove a piece of beef from the brine crock, being certain that the remaining beef in the crock is still covered with brine. Rinse off and cover with cold water. Simmer 3 to 4 hours, until tender. Drain off liquid and add 1 quart fresh water. Bring almost to a boil and add six small potatoes that have been scrubbed but not peeled. Simmer over low heat ½ hour, then add 2 cups shredded cabbage over the top. Simmer another ½ hour, then serve, right in the pot, to 4 to 6 people.

Brined Fish Chowder:
Remove the fish from the brine and wash. Cut in two-inch lengths. Tear these in pieces and cover with cold water. Soak 3 to 4 hours. Rinse off a small slice of brined fat pork and slice it into small pieces. Brown in a pan over low heat. Add 1 tablespoon flour and stir in the accumulated fat in the pan until smooth. Add 1 quart of cold water, the fish, 1 tablespoon diced dried onion, 1 tablespoon diced, dried green pepper and 1½ cups diced raw potato. Simmer over low heat until potatoes and fish are tender. Add 2 cups milk and season with pepper to taste. Do not add salt without tasting. Serves 4.

DRYING HERBS

Herbs are plants from which the leaves, seeds, flowers or roots — and often more than one of these — are used for flavor or aroma. Many herbs are used in the vegetable garden, also, to repel harmful insects.

Most herbs are used fresh during the summer months. A few, such as chives and parsley, are best grown in window pots during the winter season. But most may be dried for winter use with good results.

The time for harvesting depends upon the part of the plant used for flavor. Flowers are most flavorful before they are fully in bloom, when the petals are beginning to open.

Leaves are best dried when they are young and tender and most aromatic. Seeds should be harvested when their color changes from green to brown or gray, but before the pods burst and the seeds begin to fall to the ground. Herb roots are usually dug in the fall, when the plant has reached its full growth and flavor.

Because their flavor is delicate and easily dissipated by heat, herbs are best dried naturally, in a well-shaded, well-ventilated spot, sometimes even in the dark. The tender-leafed herbs such as basil, costmary, tarragon and mint are best dried in semi-darkness to retain their green color.

To dry herb leaves, pick them as soon as the morning dew is gone, selecting the youngest, most tender leaves. Discard any that are dirty, but do not wash. Spread on cheesecloth-covered trays and place in a well-ventilated, not-too-sunny room. If they are left in the shade out of doors, it will be necessary to cover with a thin layer of cheesecloth.

When the leaves are dry, separate them from the stalks and remove the ribs if necessary, then crush in the hands or with a rolling pin. The exception is bay leaves, which are left whole. Store crushed or pulverized leaves in tightly sealed jars in a dark place.

Flowers are hung upside down, on the stem, in a dark, well-ventilated place until thoroughly dry. For most uses the petals are then plucked from the flowers and dried on trays.

Herb roots are cut into slices or chunks and dried on trays in the shade or hung on a cord in an attic or high under a porch. A few, as noted later, are dried in the sun. Horseradish root is not dried.

Herb seeds are partially dried on the stalk, then separated from the seed pod and spread on trays to finish drying, then stored in sealed jars.

Dried herbs may be used without soaking. Simply add them to the food with which they are to be used. Keep in mind, however, that dried herbs have three to four times the potence of fresh herbs. Use them sparingly.

Following are some suggested uses for herbs which are often grown in home gardens. Some are more easily grown in the southern states, but may be started indoors in the North. All may be grown in temperate zones. In parenthesis is the part of the plant used for flavoring or aroma.

ANGELICA: (leaf) (stem) (root) (seed) Roots and tender stems are candied and used in cookies and cakes. Stems are added to cooked vegetables. Fresh leaves are used to flavor salads, fresh fruits, jams and jellies. Dried seed may be added to cake or cookie dough.

ANISE: (seed) A licorice-flavored seed similar to caraway. Used in herb tea, sprinkled on sweet rolls or added to cookie batter.

BASIL: (leaf) Also known as Sweet Basil. Dried basil may be used to flavor tomato or potato dishes, vegetable juices, cheese and egg mixtures, soups, fish, beef, lamb, poultry and venison, salads and vegetables.

BAY: (leaf) Grown only in warm climates, mature bay leaves may be picked and dried at any time. A versatile herb, it is used to flavor meat, gravy, fish, game, poultry, shellfish, salads, soups, stews and cooked vegetables.

BERGAMOT: (leaf) Also known as Bee Balm or Lemon Balm. The delicate lemon flavor of the fresh or dried leaves is used in iced tea, as an herb tea, in lemonade, and to flavor fruits and salads. The dried leaves are used with roast meats, in creamed soups and as a poultry seasoning.

BORAGE: (leaf) (stem) (flower) A subtly cucumber-flavored plant. Tender sprigs of fresh borage may be used as parsley, the stems may be used as a vegetable, the flowers used to flavor lemonade or fruit punch. Stems and leaves may be candied for use in cookies and cakes. Dried leaves are sprinkled on cooked vegetables.

BURNET: (leaf) Fresh leaves are used in salads. Dried leaves are used to flavor vinegar or in herb tea.

CALENDULA: (flower) Dried flower petals are used in salads, in stews, fish chowders or with game.

CAMOMILE: (flower) Dried camomile petals are used for herb tea.

CARAWAY: (seed) (leaf) (root) Dried caraway seeds are used to add flavor and crunch to cheese, breads, cookies and cakes, are cooked with sauerkraut and added to coleslaw. Fresh leaves are used to flavor salads, cooked vegetables, roast pork or cream cheese. The roots are eaten cooked, as a parsnip-tasting vegetable.

CATNIP: (leaf) Leaves are used, fresh or dried, as a seasoning in salads. Catnip tea is brewed from the dried leaf.

CELERY: (seed) (leaf) (root) Usually thought of as a vegetable, celery is truly an herb. The leaves, fresh or dried, are used to flavor soups, stews or tomato dishes. The root is cooked fresh as a vegetable or used as flavoring. The dried seed flavors sandwich spreads, salads, pickles and relishes.

CHERVIL: (leaf) (root) Dried chervil leaves are used to season fish and chicken dishes. Fresh leaves are added to salads. Roots are cooked and served as a vegetable.

CHIVES: (leaf) Fresh or dried chive leaves add a mild onion flavor to salads, cottage cheese, scrambled eggs and cream sauces.

CORIANDER: (seed) (leaf) Dried seed is crushed or ground and used to flavor potato salad, bread, cookies, pumpkin pie, meats, sausages and fruit dishes. Leaves are used fresh or dried in soups and stews.

COSTMARY: (leaf) The long, fragrant leaves are pulled

in early spring and dried away from light. Dried or fresh leaves are used to flavor meat and game. Dried leaves are used for herb tea.

CUMIN: (seed) An ingredient of chili powder, cumin seed is used to flavor sausage, meats, fish and game. May be used sparingly in cheese and breads.

DILL: (seed) (flower) (leaf) Dill flowers are used to flavor pickles and dilled vegetables. Although best used fresh, they may be dried when the flower still has some unopened buds. Leaves and stems, dried or fresh, are chopped fine and used in salads, meat dishes, soups and stews. Dried seeds are used for pickling, in coleslaw or cream sauces, on cooked vegetables and in meat dishes. Flowers, leaves or seeds may be used to make dill vinegar.

FENNEL: (leaf) (seed) Also known as Florence Fennel, fresh and dried fennel leaves are used for flavoring in soups and casseroles. Dried seed is used for cookies and desserts or ground for use in cheese and meat dishes.

GARLIC: (root) Used sparingly, one of the most versatile of all seasonings. Root is seasoned, not thoroughly dried, for winter keeping. Use to flavor almost any meat, salad, meat or egg dish for flavoring vinegar or salad dressings. (See also section on Sun Drying.)

GINGER: (root) Roots of the wild or cultivated ginger plants are dried in the sun, then ground for seasoning in cookies, cakes, pumpkin pies and puddings.

HOREHOUND: (leaf) Fresh leaves are used to make candy. Dried leaves are used to flavor honey and for herb tea.

HORSERADISH: (root) Horseradish root is not dried, but is ground while fresh to make a hot condiment to use with fish, game, beef, lamb and poultry. Young leaves may be used as a cooked vegetable.

HYSSOP: (leaf) (flower) Dried flowers are used to

flavor soups, stews and for herb tea. Leaves are dried to be used in vegetable or cranberry juice.

LAVENDER: (flower) Usually is used dried in sachets and for dried flower arrangements. Dried lavender flowers are sometimes used to flavor desserts, beverages and salads.

LEMON VERBENA: (leaf) Dried leaves are used to flavor fruits or beverages or to make herb tea.

LOVAGE: (leaf) (seed) (root) The leaves, seeds and roots of this celery-flavored plant are dried to flavor soups, stews, sauces and casseroles.

MAJORAM:(leaf) Also known as Sweet Marjoram, dried, pulverized marjoram leaves are used to season meat dishes, sausage, vegetables, fish, chicken and game.

MINT: (leaf) Including spearmint and peppermint. Dried mint leaves are used for herb tea. Fresh mint leaves are used for mint sauce, jellies and cooling drinks.

MUSTARD: (leaf) (seed) The leaf is used fresh as a cooked vegetable or in salads. The dried whole seed is used in pickling, or ground and blended with vinegar as a condiment.

OREGANO: (leaf) (flower) Just as the flower begins to open, the leaves and flowers are cut and dried quickly, then crushed for use in tomato dishes and with game.

PARSLEY: (leaf) Rich in Vitamin C and reasonably so in Vitamin A, fresh or dried parsley is added to cooked vegetables, soups, salads, meat, fish or egg dishes and chopped fine to garnish sauces. (See also sections on Sun and Artificial Drying.)

POPPY: (seed) Dried seed is sprinkled on French bread, rolls and cookies before baking.

ROSE: (flower) Dried flower petals are used to flavor jams and jellies, baked fruits and herb teas.

ROSEMARY: (leaf) Dried leaves are used to flavor meat, soups, dressing, game, vegetables, meat and fruit salads and meat sauces.

RUE: (leaf) Dried leaves are added sparingly to vegetable juices, stews, soups and to beef or lamb.

SAGE: (leaf) Dried leaves are used to flavor cheese, poultry, sausage, dressing, omelets, meat loaves and sauces.

SASSAFRAS: (leaf) (flower) (root) (bark) Almost any portion of the sassafras tree may be used fresh or dried to make a delicious herb tea. Dried leaves are also used in soups and to flavor vegetables.

SAVORY: (leaf) Winter and Summer Savory. Dried leaves are used to flavor dressings, salads, stews, beans and dried peas, cabbage or sauerkraut, vegetable juices, game and poultry.

SESAME: (seed) Dried sesame seed is used in cakes, cookies and breads.

SORREL: (leaf) Dried sorrel leaves add flavor to soups, stews, omelets, cooked vegetables and casseroles.

TANSY: (flower) (leaf) Dried tansy leaves are crushed and added to omelets, fish and meat dishes or brewed into an herb tea. Also is grown as an insect repellant.

TARRAGON: (leaf) Dried tarragon leaves give flavor to roast meats, steaks and poultry. Tarragon vinegar is made from fresh leaves.

THYME: (leaf) (flower) Dried thyme leaves are used in soups, stews, chowders and meat dishes, egg and game dishes. The dried flowers are used in sachets and for herb tea.

WOODRUFF: (leaf) Also known as Sweet Woodruff, the dried leaves are used to flavor wines, in herb tea and in sachets.

CONTENTS
INDEX

Blanching
 hot water method   9, 10, 11
 steam method   9, 10, 11
Brined Foods
 Cooking:
  brined fish & meats   48, 49
  brined vegetables   48

 General directions   45
 Preserving:
  beef   46
  beets   47
  butter   47
  carrots   47
  cauliflower   48
  corn   47
  green beans   46
  pork   45, 46
  venison   46

Drying Foods, Artificial Method
 (see also Fish, Fruits, Meats,
 Vegetables)
 equipment   5, 24
 general directions   8, 9, 24, 25
 ready tests (see each food)
 stove-top drier   6, 7, 8
 temperatures   24
Drying Foods, Sunlight Method
 (see also Fish, Fruits, Meat,
 Vegetables)
 Equipment   5, 12
 General directions   8, 9, 11, 12
 location   12
 ready tests (see each food)

Eggs, Drying
 whites   34
 whole   34
 yolks   34
Eggs, Dried
 cooking directions   43, 44, 45

Fish, Brined (see Brined Foods)
Fish, Dried
 cooking recipes   44
Fish, Drying
 general directions   32, 33
Fruit Papers or Leathers
 Sunlight drying:
  apples   35
  apricots   35
  peaches   35
  plums   35
  mixed fruits   36
Fruits, Dried
 general cooking directions
  recipes   36
Fruits, Drying, Artificial Method
  apples   25
  apricots   26
  blueberries   26
  cherries   26
  currants   27
  figs   27
  peaches   28
  pears   28
  raspberries   29
  rhubarb   29
  strawberries   30
Fruits, Drying, Sunlight Method
  apples   13
  apricots   13, 14
  bananas   14
  blueberries   15
  candied fruits   15
  cherries   16
  currants   17
  figs   17
  lemon peel   18
  peaches   19, 20
  pears   20
  plums   21
  prunes   21

57

raspberries   22
rhubarb   22
strawberries   23

Herbs
drying methods   50
fresh uses   49
harvesting times   49, 50
storage methods   50
Uses:
  angelica   51
  anise   51
  basil   51
  bay   51
  bergamot   51
  borage   51
  burnet   52
  calendula   52
  camomile   52
  caraway   52
  caraway   52
  catnip   52
  celery   52
  chervil   52
  chives   52
  coriander   52
  costmary   52
  cumin   53
  dill   53
  fennel   53
  garlic   53, 17, 18
  ginger   53
  horehound   53
  horseradish   53
  hyssop   53
  lavender   54
  lemon verbena   54
  lovage   54
  marjoram   54
  mint   54
  mustard   54
  oregano   54

parsley   19, 28, 54
poppy   54
rose   54
rosemary   54
rue   55
sage   55
sassafras   55
savory   55
sesame   55
sorrel   55
tansey   55
tarragon   55
thyme   55
woodruff   55
Meats, Brined (see Brined Foods)
Meats, Dried
  Cooking recipes   43, 44
Meats, Drying
  general directions   31
    beef or ham   31
    brined beef   31
    cured beef   31, 32
    pork   32
    poultry   33
    small game   33
    venison   32
Milk, Dried
  cooking directions   45
Milk, Drying
  general directions   33, 34

Storage
  materials   11
  methods   11

Vegetables, Brined (see Brined Foods)
Vegetables, Dried
  cooking directions   36
  cooking recipes   40-41
  soup recipes   41-43

Vegetables, Drying, Artificial Method
    beans   26
    beets   26
    carrots   26
    corn   27
    green beans   27
    lima beans   27
    parsley   28
    peas   28
    peppers   28
    pumpkin   28, 29
    rhubarb   29
    rutabaga   30
    soybeans   29
    squash   30
    tomatoes   30
    turnips   30

Vegetables, Drying, Sunlight Method
    beans   14, 15
    beets   15
    carrots   15
    corn   16, 17
    mock figs   17
    garlic   17, 18
    green beans   18
    lima beans   18
    mushrooms   18, 19
    onions   19
    parsley   19
    parsnips   19
    peas   20
    peppers   20, 21
    pumpkins   21, 22
    rhubarb   22
    rutabaga   22
    soybeans   22
    squash   23
    tomatoes   23, 24
    turnips   24

NOTES